A SHAMBHALA THRESHOLD BOOK

RUMI
DAYLIGHT

A Daybook of Spiritual Guidance

SHAMBHALA
Boston & London
1999

SHAMBHALA PUBLICATIONS, INC.
Horticultural Hall
300 Massachusetts Avenue
Boston, Massachusetts 02115
www.shambhala.com

Printed in the United States of America
∞ This edition is printed on acid-free paper
that meets the American National Standards Institute Z39.48 Standard.
Distributed in the United States by Random House, Inc.,
and in Canada by Random House of Canada Ltd

Library of Congress Cataloging-in -Publications Data

Jalāl al-Dīn Rūmī, Maulana, 1207–1273.
　　　　　[Masnavī. Book 1–2. English. Selections]
　　　　　Rumi—daylight: a daybook of spiritual guidance.
　　　　　　　　　p.　　　cm.
　　　　　Translation by Camille Adams Helminski and Edmund Kabir Helminski
of selected verses from Masnavi, book 1–2.
　　　　　Includes index.
　　　　　ISBN 1–57062–530–1 (paper)
　　　　　1. Sufi poetry, Persian Translations into English. I. Helminski,
Kabir, 1947– . II. Helminski, Camille Adams, 1951– .
III. Title. IV. Title: Daylight.
PK6481.M8E2　　　　　　1999
891'.5511—dc21　　　　　　　　　　　　　　　　99–32290
　　　　　　　　　　　　　　　　　　　　　　　　　　　　　CIP

BVG 01

Contents

Preface

AFTER eleven years of turning to the *Mathnawi* of Jelaluddin Rumi for "light," the idea came that this light might be made more readily available to more people in the format of a "daybook." *Rumi: Daylight* comes to you as an offering, as a tool, as a possible source of insight and refreshment, support and encouragement. It may be used from the first day of the year to the last to deepen a whole cycle or at special moments, opened randomly. May your hand be guided as you turn the pages; and may the voice within these words soothe and strengthen your soul. For the way is only difficult until it becomes easy. Moments of ease, though, may come and go numerous times before one arrives and learns to live in a new land.

The verses are presented here in the order in which they would be found within Books I and II, which hold roughly a third of the 25,632 lines of the whole six books of the *Mathnawi*. Although other possibilities presented themselves, keeping true to the pattern woven in the *Mathnawi* seemed best.

As when one walks along the shore of the ocean, one finds treasures in the sand, so here, too, one may look down and discover a precious piece to hold close for awhile. In making this selection, I attempted to choose short sections that would stand alone and elucidate our lives. I recognize though that any selection is limited to time and place, and that were I to journey through the same two books of the *Mathnawi* now, I might surface with different lines to share with you, or if you made that journey yourself, you might choose different words. Those published here are a beginning and will, I hope, give a strong taste of the guidance and wisdom that comes through the vehicle of Mevlana Jelaluddin Rumi, may God preserve his secret, and help us all to recognize

> *the shop of Oneness,*
> *the Ocean that has many harbors,*
> *yet where there is no division*
> *between man and man, or woman,*
> *but only a unity of souls*
> *in the process of return to their Creator,*
> *Whose breath lives inside each one*
> *and helps to guide us home.*

Many thanks flow out to all who have lent support to this project--many helping hands and hearts have been involved in the process, among them are Lora Gobel, Tom Goldberg and George Witterschein who helped in editing. What a blessing it has been to work together with my husband, Kabir. We are grateful for the extensive groundwork established by R.A. Nicholson in his full translation of the six books of the *Mathnawi*. Kabir and I hope to continue our work with the *Mathnawi* and bring kernels from the remaining four books to you soon.

Continually sustaining us has been the presence of Sheikh Suleyman Hayati Dede, may God preserve his secret. He mirrored to us in reality the beauty and breadth of Mevlana Jelauluddin Rumi, witness of God. May we take Mevlana as an example and open to the whisper of God in our own hearts that our words, too, may become fragrant and full of nourishment.

Camille Adams Helminski
Putney, Vermont
1990

Introduction

I N the last decades of the Twentieth Century the spiritual influence of Mevlana Jelaluddin Rumi is being strongly felt by people of diverse beliefs throughout the Western world. He is being recognized here in the West, as he has been for seven centuries in the Middle East and Western Asia, as one of the greatest literary and spiritual figures of all time.

Different qualities of Rumi have been brought forth by a variety of new translations that have appeared during the nineteen-eighties. He has been presented as both refined and sensual, sober and ecstatic, deeply serious and extremely funny, rarefied and accessible. It is a sign of his profound universality that he has been so many things to so many people.

It is our wish in this book to begin to present his spiritual teachings concisely and comprehensively, to offer some jewels from this vast treasure.

Jelaluddin Rumi was born in 1207 in Balkh in what is today Afghanistan. At an early age his family left Balkh because of the danger of the invading Mongols and settled in Konya, Turkey, which was then the capital of the Seljuk Empire. His father Bahauddin was a great religious teacher who received a position at the university in Konya.

Mevlana's early spiritual education was under the tutelage of his father Bahauddin and later under his father's close friend Sayyid Burhaneddin of Balkh. The circumstances surrounding Sayyid's undertaking the education of his friend's son are interesting: Sayyid had been in Balkh, Afghanistan when he felt the death of his friend Bahauddin and realized that he must go to Konya to take over Jelaluddin's spiritual education. He came to Konya when Mevlana was about twenty-four years old, and for nine years instructed him in "the science of the prophets and states," beginning with a strict forty day retreat and continuing with various disciplines of meditation and fasting. During this time Jelaluddin also spent more than four years in Aleppo and Damascus studying with some of the greatest religious minds of the time.

As the years passed, Mevlana grew both in knowledge and consciousness of God. Eventually Sayyid Burhaneddin felt that he had fulfilled his responsibility toward Jelaluddin, and he wanted to live out the rest of his years in seclusion. He told Mevlana, "You are now ready, my son. You have no equal in any of the branches of learning. You have become a lion of knowledge. I am such a lion myself and we are not both needed here and that is why I want to go. Furthermore, a great friend will come to you, and you will be each other's mirror. He will lead you to the innermost parts of the spiritual world, just as you will lead him. Each of you will complete the other, and you will be the greatest friends in the entire world." And so Sayyid intimated the coming of Shams of Tabriz, the central event of Rumi's life.

At the age of thirty-seven Mevlana met the spiritual vagabond Shams. Much has already been written about their relationship. Prior to this encounter Rumi had been an eminent professor of religion and a highly attained mystic; after this he became an inspired poet and a great lover of humanity. Rumi's meeting with Shams can be compared to Abraham's meeting with Melchizidek. I owe to Murat Yagan this explanation: "A Melchizidek and a Shams are messengers from the Source. They do nothing themselves but carry enlightenment to someone who can receive it, someone who is either too full or too empty. Mevlana was one who was too full. After receiving it, he could apply this message for the benefit of humanity." Shams was burning and Rumi caught fire. Shams' companionship with

Rumi was brief. Despite the fact that each was a perfect mirror for the other Shams disappeared, not once but twice. The first time, Rumi's son Sultan Veled searched for and discovered him in Damascus. The second disappearance, however, proved to be final, and it is believed that he may have been murdered by people who resented his influence over Mevlana.

Rumi was a man of knowledge and sanctity before meeting Shams, but only after the alchemy of this relationship was he able to fulfill Sayyid Burhaneddin's prediction that he would "drown men's souls in a fresh life and in the immeasurable abundance of God . . . and bring to life the dead of this false world with . . . meaning and love."

For more than ten years after meeting Shams, Mevlana had been spontaneously composing odes, or ghazals, and these had been collected in a large volume called the *Divan-i Kabir*. Meanwhile Mevlana had developed a deep spiritual friendship with Husameddin Chelebi. The two of them were wandering through the Meram vineyards outside of Konya one day when Husameddin described an idea he had to Mevlana: "If you were to write a book like the *Ilahiname* of Sanai or the *Mantik'ut-Tayr'i* of Fariduddin Attar it would become the companion of many troubadours. They would fill their hearts from your work and compose music to accompany it."

Mevlana smiled and took from inside the folds of his turban a piece of paper on which were written the opening eighteen lines of his *Mathnawi*, beginning with:

> Listen to the reed and the tale it tells,
> how it sings of separation. . .

Husameddin wept for joy and implored Mevlana to write volumes more. Mevlana replied, "Chelebi, if you consent to write for me, I will recite." And so it happened that Mevlana in his early fifties began the dictation of this monumental work. As

Husameddin described the process: "He never took a pen in his hand while composing the *Mathnawi*. Wherever he happened to be, whether in the school, at the Ilgin hot springs, in the Konya baths, or in the Meram vineyards, I would write down what he recited. Often I could barely keep up with his pace, sometimes, night and day for several days. At other times he would not compose for months, and once for two years there was nothing. At the completion of each book I would read it back to him, so that he could correct what had been written."

The *Mathnawi* can justifiably be considered the greatest spiritual masterpiece ever written by a human being. Its content includes the full spectrum of life on earth, every kind of human activity: religious, cultural, political, sexual, domestic; every kind of human character from the vulgar to the refined; as well as copious and specific details of the natural world, history and geography. It is also a book that presents the vertical dimension of life-- from this mundane world of desire, work, and things, to the most sublime levels of metaphysics and cosmic awareness. It is its completeness that enchants us.

What do we need to know to receive the knowledge that Rumi offers us?

First of all, it needs to be understood that Rumi's tradition is not an "Eastern" tradition. It is neither of the East nor the West, but something in between. Rumi's mother-tongue was Persian, an Indo-European language strongly influenced by Semitic (Arabic) vocabulary, something like French with a smattering of Hebrew.

Furthermore, the Islamic tradition, which shaped him, acknowledges that only one religion has been given to mankind through countless prophets, or messengers, who have come to every people on earth bearing this knowledge of Spirit. God is the subtle source of all life, Whose essence cannot be described or compared to anything, but Who can be known through the spiritual qualities that are manifest in the world and in the human heart. It is a deeply mystical tradition, on the one hand, with a strong and clear emphasis on human dignity and social justice, on the other.

Islam is understood as a continuation of the Judeo-Christian or Abrahamic tradition, honoring the Hebrew prophets, as well as Jesus and Mary. Muslims, however, are very sensitive to the issue of attributing divinity to a human being, which they see as the primary error of Christianity. Although Jesus is called in the Qur'an "the Spirit of God," it would be thought a blasphemy to identify any human being exclusively as God. Muhammed is viewed as the last of those human prophets who brought the message of God's love.

In Rumi's world, the Islamic way of life had established a high level of spiritual awareness among the general population. The average person would be someone who performed regular ablutions and prayed five times a day, fasted from food and drink during the daylight hours for at least one month a year, and closely followed a code which emphasized the continual remembrance of God, intention, integrity, generosity, and respect for all life. Although the *Mathnawi* can appeal to us on many levels, it assumes a rather high level of spiritual awareness as a starting point and extends to the very highest levels of spiritual understanding.

The unenlightened human state is one of "faithlessness" in which an individual lives in slavery to the false self and the desires of the material world. The spiritual practices which Rumi would have known were aimed at transforming the compulsiveness of the false self and attaining Islam or "Submission" to a higher order of reality. Without this Submission the real self is enslaved to the ego and lives in a state of internal conflict due to the contradictory impulses of the ego. The enslaved ego is cut off from the heart, the chief organ for perceiving reality, and cannot receive the spiritual guidance and nourishment which the heart provides.

Overcoming this enslavement and false separation leads to the realization and development of our true humanity. Spiritual maturity is the realization that the self is a reflection of the Divine. God is the Beloved or Friend, the transpersonal identity. Love of God leads to the lover forgetting himself in the love of the Beloved.

All of the material in this volume is taken from the first two books of Rumi's *Mathnawi*, the whole of which comprises six books and 25,632 couplets. In Rumi's own words which preface Book One, the *Mathnawi* is "the roots of the roots of the roots of the roots of the Religion, unveiling the mysteries of attainment and certainty; and which is the greatest science of God and the clearest way of God and the most manifest evidence of God. It is the heart's paradise, having fountains and boughs. . . Within it the righteous eat and drink, and the free rejoice and are happy; and like the Nile of Egypt it is a refreshment to those who patiently endure, but a grief to the people of Pharoah and the faithless. . . It is the cure of hearts, and the purge of sorrows, and the interpreter of the Qur'an, and an abundant source of gifts, and the cleansing of character. . . since God observes it and protects it, *'and He is the best guardian and He is the most merciful of them that show mercy.*" So says this feeble slave who is in need of God's mercy."

Edmund Kabir Helminski
Putney, Vermont
1990

---

* *Whenever a phrase or sentence is italicized in this book, it signifies that Rumi is quoting directly from the Qur'an.*

Dedicated to Suleyman Hayati Dede
who brought us the breath of Mevlana

God, in spite of the skeptics,
caused spiritual gardens with sweet flowers to grow
in the hearts of His friends.
Every rose that is sweet-scented within,
that rose is telling of the secrets of the Universal.
Their scent, to the confusion of the skeptics,
spreads around the world, rending the veil.

[I, 2021-3]

The Beloved is all, the lover just a veil.
The Beloved is living, the lover a dead thing.
If Love witholds its strengthening care,
the lover is left like a bird without wings.
How will I be awake and aware
if the light of the Beloved is absent?
Love wills that this Word be brought forth.
If you find the mirror of the heart dull,
the rust has not been cleared from its face.

[I, 34]

Let's ask God to help us to self-control:
for one who lacks it, lacks His Grace.

[I, 78]

The undisciplined man doesn't wrong himself alone—
he sets fire to the whole world.
Discipline enabled Heaven to be filled with light;
discipline enabled the angels to be immaculate and holy.

[I, 79; 91]

Suspicion and greed at the table of Majesty are ingratitude.

[I, 86]

The lover's ailment is not like any other;
Love is the astrolabe of God's mysteries.
Whether Love is from heaven or earth,
it points to God.

[I, 110-111]

My friend, the sufi is the son of the present moment:
to say "tomorrow" is not our way.

[I, 134]

A thorn in the foot is hard to find.
What about a thorn in the heart?
If everyone saw the thorn in his heart,
when would sorrow gain the upper hand?

[I, 152-3]

When your heart becomes the grave of your secret,
that desire of yours will be gained more quickly.
The Prophet said that anyone
who keeps secret his inmost thought
will soon attain the object of his desire.
When seeds are buried in the earth,
their inward secrets become the flourishing garden.

[I, 175-7]

There are true promises that make the heart grateful;
there are false promises, fraught with disquiet.
The promise of the noble is sterling;
the promise of the unworthy breeds anguish of the soul.

[I, 180-1]

The peacock's plumage is his enemy.
Many a king has been slain by his magnificence.

[I, 208]

The world is the mountain,
and each action, the shout that echoes back.

[I, 215]

Love of the dead does not last,
because the dead will not return.
But love of the living
is in every moment fresher than a bud,
both to the inward and the outward eye.
Choose the love of that Living One
who is everlasting, who offers you
the wine that increases life.
Do not say, "We have no entrance to that King."
Dealings with the generous are not difficult.

[I, 217-9; 221]

This discipline and rough treatment are a furnace
to extract the silver from the dross.
This testing purifies the gold
by boiling the scum away.

[I, 232-3]

The spiritual path wrecks the body
and afterwards restores it to health.
It destroys the house to unearth the treasure,
and with that treasure builds it better than before.

[I, 306-7]

Anger and lust make a man squint;
they cloud the spirit so it strays from truth.
When self-interest appears, virtue hides:
a hundred veils rise between the heart and the eye.

[I, 333-4]

Hear one of the sayings related from the Prophet:
"No prayer is complete without Presence."

[I, 381]

Though there be a thousand snares at our feet,
when You are with us there is no difficulty.

[I, 387]

The more awake one is to the material world,
the more one is asleep to spirit.
When our soul is asleep to God,
other wakefulness closes the door of Divine grace.

[I, 409-410]

On the way there is no harder pass than this:
fortunate is he who does not carry envy as a companion.

[I, 431]

The soil is faithful to its trust:
whatever you have sown in it, you reap the same.
But until springtime brings the touch of God,
the soil does not reveal its secrets.

[I, 509; 511]

When He Himself is the light of your eye,
a hundred worlds like ours appear.
If this one looks bottomless and vast,
remember: to Omnipotence it is less than an atom.

[I, 523-6]

How long will you say, "I will conquer the whole world
and fill it with myself"?
Even if snow covered the world completely,
the sun could melt it with a glance.
A single spark of God's mercy
can turn poison into springwater.
Where there is doubt,
He establishes certainty.

[I, 542-6]

If ten lamps are present in one place,
each differs in form from another;
yet you can't distinguish whose radiance is whose
when you focus on the light.
In the field of spirit there is no division;
no individuals exist.
Sweet is the oneness of the Friend with His friends.
Catch hold of spirit.
Help this headstrong self disintegrate;
that beneath it you may discover unity,
like a buried treasure.

[I, 678-83]

Don't take a wooden sword into battle.
Go, find one of steel;
then march forward with joy.
The sword of reality is the saint's protection:
your time with him
is worth as much as the cup of life itself.
All the wise have said the same:
the one who knows God
is God's mercy to His creatures.

[I, 714-7]

Companionship with the holy, makes you one of them.
Though you're rock or marble, you'll become a jewel
when you reach the man of heart.

[I, 721-2]

Plant the love of the holy ones within your spirit;
don't give your heart to anything
but the love of those whose hearts are glad.
Don't go to the neighborhood of despair:
there is hope.
Don't go in the direction of darkness:
suns exist.

[I, 723-4]

Feed your heart in conversation
with someone harmonious with it;
seek spiritual advancement from one who is advanced.

[I, 726]

God has scattered His light over all souls;
happy are they who have held up their skirts to receive it.
Those lucky ones don't look to anything but God;
without that skirt of love,
we miss our share.

[I, 760-2]

The idol of your self is the mother of all idols.
The material idol is only a snake;
while this inner idol is a dragon.
It is easy to break an idol,
but to regard the self as easy to subdue is a mistake.

[I, 772; 778]

Sometimes, in order to help, He makes us miserable;
but heartache for His sake brings happiness.
Laughter will come after tears.
Whoever foresees this is a servant blessed by God.
Wherever water flows, life flourishes:
wherever tears fall, Divine mercy is shown.

[I, 817-20]

Weep like the waterwheel,
that green herbs may spring up
from the courtyard of your soul.
If you wish for tears,
have mercy on one who sheds tears;
if you wish mercy, show mercy to the weak.

[I, 821-2]

When you feel pain, ask pardon of God;
this pain has its uses.
When He pleases, pain becomes joy;
bondage itself becomes freedom.
When you take a clear look,
you'll see that from God
are both the water of mercy and the fire of anger.

[I, 836-7; 852]

Water and clay, when fed on the breath of Jesus,
spread wings, became a bird and flew.
Your praise of God is a breath
from your body of water and clay.
Make it a bird of paradise
by breathing into it your heart's sincerity.

[I, 866-7]

Pay attention to the significance of
"He who works is beloved of God."
Through trusting God
don't become neglectful of ways and means.

[I, 914]

Since our vision is so limited, let's go!
Let our sight be dissolved in the seeing of the Friend.
Our sight for His—what an exchange!

[I, 921-2]

The world is a prison and we are the prisoners:
dig a hole in the prison and let yourself out!

[I, 982]

Water in the boat is the ruin of the boat,
but water under the boat is its support.
Since Solomon cast the desire for wealth out from his heart,
he didn't call himself by any name but "poor."
The stoppered jar, though in rough water,
floated because of its empty heart.
When the wind of poverty is in anyone,
she floats in peace on the waters of this world.

[I, 985-8]

Refresh your faith, but not with talking.
You have secretly refreshed your desires.
As long as desires are fresh, faith is not;
for it is these desires that lock that gate.

[I, 1078-9]

The light which shines in the eye
is really the light of the heart.
The light which fills the heart
is the light of God, which is pure
and separate from the light of intellect and sense.

[I, 1126-7]

God created pain and sorrow
that happiness might show itself by contrast.
For hidden things are made manifest
by means of their opposites:
since God has no opposite, He is hidden.

[I, 1130-1]

Form came forth from formlessness
and returned there, for *verily unto Him are we returning.*
Every instant, we are dying and returning:
the Prophet declared that this world is but a moment.
Our thought is an arrow shot from Him into the air.
How shall it stay in the air?
It comes back to God.

[I, 1141-3]

To speak the same language is kinship and affinity:
when you're with those in whom you can't confide,
you're like a prisoner in chains.
Many Indians and Turks speak the same tongue;
yet many pairs of Turks find they're foreigners.
The tongue of mutual understanding is quite special:
to be one of heart is better than to have a common tongue.

[I, 1205-7]

* Whenever a phrase or sentence is italicized in this book, it signifies that Rumi is
quoting directly from the Qur'an.

With us, the name of everything
is its outward appearance;
with the Creator,
the name of each thing is its inward reality.
In the eye of Moses, the name of his rod was "staff";
in the eye of the Creator, its name was "dragon."
In brief, that which we are in the end
is our real name with God.

[I, 1239-40; 1244]

Though Destiny a hundred times waylays you,
in the end it pitches a tent for you in heaven.
It is God's kindness to terrify you
in order to lead you to safety.

[I, 1260-1]

If you dig a pit for others to fall into,
you will fall into it yourself.
Don't weave yourself a silkworm's cocoon
and don't dig that pit so deep.
Don't think the weak have no protector
and say the words of the Qur'an,
When the help of God shall come.

[I, 1311-3]

Many of the faults you see in others, dear reader,
are your own nature reflected in them.
As the Prophet said,
"The faithful are mirrors to one another."

[I, 1319; 1328)

With will, fire becomes sweet water;
and without will, even water becomes fire.

[I, 1336]

The inner search is from You.
The blind are cured by Your gift.
Without our searching, You gave us this search.

[I, 1337-8]

The lion who breaks the enemy's ranks
is a minor hero
compared to the lion who overcomes himself.

[I, 1389]

Fear Not is the hospitality offered to those who fear.

[I, 1429]

O son, only those whose spiritual eye has been opened
know how compulsive we are.

[I, 1466]

Whoever gives reverence receives reverence:
whoever brings sugar eats almond cake.
Who are the good women for? The good men.
Honor your friend;
or see what happens if you don't.

[I, 1494-5]

The intellectual quest,
though fine as pearl or coral,
is not the spiritual search.
That spiritual search is on another level.
Spiritual wine is a different substance.

[I, 1501-2]

We owe thankfulness to God,
not sour faces.

[I, 1525]

Each moment contains
a hundred messages from God:
To every cry of "Oh Lord,"
He answers a hundred times, "I am here."

[I, 1578]

The intelligent desire self-control;
children want candy.

[I, 1601-2]

Since in order to speak, one must first listen,
learn to speak by listening.

[I, 1627]

When, with just a taste,
envy and deceit arise,
and ignorance and forgetfulness are born,
know you have tasted the unlawful.

[I, 1645]

That taste is the seed, and thoughts are its fruits:
that taste is the sea, and thoughts are its pearls.
Eating lawful food gives birth to
the inclination to serve God
and the resolve to go to His world.

[I, 1647-8]

Know that a word suddenly shot from the tongue
is like an arrow shot from the bow.
Son, that arrow won't turn back on its way;
you must damn a torrent at the source.

[I, 1658-9]

O tongue, you are an endless treasure.
O tongue, you are also an endless disease.

[I, 1702]

I am burning.
If any one lacks tinder,
let him set his rubbish ablaze with my fire.

[I, 1721]

Dam the torrent of ecstasy when it runs in flood,
so that it won't bring shame and ruin.
But why should I fear ruin?
Under the ruin waits a royal treasure.
He that is drowned in God wishes to be more drowned.
While his spirit is tossed up and down
by the waves of the sea,
he asks, "Is the bottom of the sea more delightful, or the top?
Is the Beloved's arrow more fascinating, or the shield?"
O heart, if you recognize any difference
between joy and sorrow,
these lies will tear you apart.
Although your desire tastes sweet,
doesn't the Beloved desire you
to be desireless?
The life of lovers is in death:
you will not win the Beloved's heart
unless you lose your own.

[I, 1743-9; 51]

Do right, You who are the glory of the just.
You, Soul, who are liberated from "we" and "I,"
     subtle spirit in man and woman.
When man and woman become one, that one is You,
     and when that one is obliterated, there You are.
Where is this "we" and this "I"? By the side of the Beloved.
     You made this "we" and "I"
in order to play this game of service with Yourself—
     that You and I might become one soul
     and in the end drown in the Beloved.

[I, 1783-4]

Can the heart possessed by laughter or grief,
tell me now, can it possibly see You at all?
Such a heart has only these borrowed things to live with.
The garden of Love is green without limit
and yields many fruits other than sorrow or joy.
Love is beyond either condition:
without spring, without autumn, it is always fresh.

[I, 1792-4]

We are bees, and our bodies are the honeycomb:
we have made the body, cell by cell, like beeswax.

[I, 1813]

Whatever the soul in man and woman strives to do,
the ear and the eye of the soul's King are at the window.

[I, 1824]

The world's flattery and hypocrisy is a sweet morsel:
eat less of it, for it is full of fire.
Its fire is hidden while its taste is manifest,
but its smoke becomes visible in the end.

[I, 1855-6]

As far as you can, be a slave, not a monarch.
Let yourself be struck. Be the ball and not the bat.

[I, 1868]

How should Spring bring forth a garden on hard stone?
Become earth, that you may grow flowers of many colors.
For you have been a heart-breaking rock.
Once, for the sake of experiment, be earth!

[I, 1911-2]

Wherever I shine the lamplight of Divine breath,
there the difficulties of a whole world are resolved.
The darkness which the earthly sun did not remove,
becomes through My breath a bright morning.

[I, 1941-2]

When a lamp has derived its light from a candle,
every one that sees the lamp certainly sees the candle.
Either behold the light of God
from the lamps of the saints,
or behold His light from the candle
of those who have gone before.

[I, 1947, 1950]

Spirit is beyond either feminine or masculine.
It is not sometimes like this and sometimes like that.

[I, 1976]

The spiritual heir of Muhammed is seated in front of you,
but where indeed is "front"?
He is before you, but where is the soul
that thinks "before"?
If you fancy you have a "before" and "behind,"
you are tied to body and deprived of spirit.
"Below" and "above," "before" and "behind,"
are attributes of the body:
the essence of the bright spirit *is*.

[I, 2006-8]

Forgetfulness of God, beloved,
is the support of this world;
spiritual intelligence its ruin.
For Intelligence belongs to that other world,
and when it prevails, this material world is overthrown.

[I, 2066-7]

If the spiritual universe and the way to it were shown,
no one for a single moment would remain.

[I, 2101]

That voice which is the origin of every cry and sound:
that indeed is the only voice, and the rest are only echoes.

[I, 2107]

Were there no men of vision,
all who are blind would be dead.

[I, 2133]

God gave me a life, the value of every single day
He alone knows.

[I, 2190]

O God, help me against this self of mine
that is seeking help from You;
I seek justice from no one but from
this justice-seeking self.
I shall not get justice from any one except from
Him who is nearer to me than myself;
For this I-ness comes moment by moment from Him.

[I, 2195-8]

You are engaged with going about,
but you are identified with your goings;
and when you come home,
you are identified with coming home.
You, whose knowledge
is without knowledge of the Giver of knowledge,
your repentence is worse than your sin.

[I, 2204-5]

It suits the generous man to give money,
but truly the generosity of the lover
is to surrender his soul.
If you give bread for God's sake,
you will be given bread in return;
if you give your life for God's sake,
you will be given life in return.

[I, 2235-6]

Some persons, relying on the promise of "tomorrow,"
have wandered for years around that door,
but "tomorrow" never comes.

[I, 2279]

Look at every animal from the gnat to the elephant:
they all are God's family
and dependent on Him for their nourishment.
What a nourisher is God!
All these griefs within our hearts
arise from the smoke and dust
of our existence and vain desires.

[I, 2295-6]

Whoever lives sweetly dies painfully:
whoever serves his body doesn't nourish his soul.

[I, 2302]

God forbid! I desire nothing from created beings:
through contentment there is
a world within my heart.

[I, 2362]

Try being poor for a day or two
and find in poverty double riches.

[I, 2373]

When the listener has become thirsty and craving,
the preacher, even if he is as good as dead,
becomes eloquent.
When the hearer is fresh and without fatigue,
the drunk and mute will find
a hundred tongues to speak.

[I, 2379-80]

Everything that is made beautiful and fair and lovely
is made for the eye of one who sees.

[I, 2383]

The love of women
is made attractive to men.
God has arranged it: how can they avoid
what God has arranged?
Inasmuch as God created woman
so that Adam might take comfort in her,
how can Adam be parted from Eve?

[I, 2425-6]

Woman is a ray of God.
She is not that earthly beloved:
she is creative, not created.

[I, 2437]

Your thinking is like a camel driver,
and you are the camel:
it drives you in every direction under its bitter control.

[I, 2497]

God connected Spirit with a body,
in order that the prophet or saint might become
a refuge for the whole world.

[I, 2521]

Love is drawing the bitter ones to the sweet,
because the foundation of all loves is righteousness.

[I, 2580]

If the saint drinks a poison it becomes an antidote,
but if the disciple drinks it,
his mind is darkened.

[I, 2602]

If love were only spiritual,
the practices of fasting and prayer would not exist.
The gifts of lovers to one another are,
in respect to love, nothing but forms;
yet, they testify
to invisible love.

[I, 2625-7]

The Prophet said that God said,
"I am not contained in the container of high and low.
I am not contained in the earth nor in all the heavens.
But I am contained in the heart of My faithful servant.
How wonderful! If you seek Me, seek Me there."

[I, 2653-5]

Don't hide Your heart but reveal it,
so that mine might be revealed,
and I might accept what I am capable of.

[I, 2682]

Abundance is seeking the beggars and the poor,
just as beauty seeks a mirror.
Beggars, then, are the mirrors of God's bounty,
and they that are with God are united with
Absolute Abundance.

[I, 2745, 2750]

Whatever knowledge the master is known to have,
with it the souls of his pupils are imbued.

[I, 2829]

Of all the things to know,
the best preparation and provision on the day of death
is the knowledge of spiritual poverty.

[I, 2834]

Though in the world you are the most learned scholar of the time
behold the vanishing of this world and this time!

[I, 2845]

Know, son, that everything in the universe
is a pitcher brimming with wisdom and beauty.
The universe is a drop of the Tigris of His Beauty,
this Beauty not contained by any skin.
His Beauty was a Hidden Treasure so full
it burst open and made the earth
more radiant than the heavens.

[I, 2860-2]

Hungry, you're a dog, angry and bad-natured.
Having eaten your fill, you become a carcass;
you lie down like a wall, senseless.
At one time a dog, at another time a carcass,
how will you run with lions, or follow the saints?

[I, 2873-5]

If you are wholly perplexed and in straits,
have patience, for patience is the key to joy.

[I, 2908]

Fast from thoughts, fast:
thoughts are like the lion and the wild ass;
men's hearts are the thickets they haunt.

[I, 2909]

Fasting is the first principle of medicine;
fast, and behold the strength of the spirit.

[I, 2911]

Without an escort you're bewildered on a familiar road;
don't travel alone on a way you haven't seen at all;
don't turn your head away from the Guide.

[I, 2944-5]

If you are irritated by every rub,
how will your mirror be polished?

[I, 2980]

Anyone in whom the troublemaking self has died,
sun and cloud obey.
As his heart is afire with knowledge and love,
the sun cannot burn him.

[I, 3004-5]

What does it mean to learn the knowledge of God's Unity?
To consume yourself in the presence of the One.
If you wish to shine like day,
burn up the night of self-existence.
Dissolve in the Being who is everything.
You grabbed hold of "I" and "we,"
and this dualism is your ruin.

[I, 3009-12]

Whosoever runs on the heels of a lion in combat,
roast meat does not fail him by day or by night.

[I, 3024]

Everything is perishing except His Face;
unless you have that Face, don't try to exist.

[I, 3052]

By God's hand, every impossible thing is made possible;
in awe of Him, the unruly settle down.

[I, 3068]

Every prophet and every saint has a way,
but all lead to God. All ways are really one.

[I, 3086]

O God, reveal to the soul
that place where speech has no letters,
so that the pure soul might go headlong
towards the expanse of nonexistence
out of which we are fed.

[I, 3092-4]

The cause of narrow mindedness is multiplicity:
the senses are drawn in many directions.
Know that the world of unification lies beyond sense:
if you want unity, march in that direction.

[I, 3099]

The wise man,
in the hour of the calamity
he took every precaution to avert,
takes warning from the death of friends.

[I, 3114]

In the presence of His Glory,
closely watch your heart
so your thoughts won't shame you.
For He sees guilt, opinion, and desire
as plainly as a hair in pure milk.

[I, 3144-5]

Someone with a clear and empty heart
mirrors images of the Invisible.
He becomes intuitive and certain
of our inmost thought,
because "the faithful are a mirror for the faithful."

[I, 3146-7]

To come empty-handed to the door of friends
is like going to the mill without wheat.

[I, 3171]

Stir a little like the fetus
that you may be given the senses
to behold the light.

[I, 3180]

What is the mirror of Being? Non-being.
Bring non-being as your gift,
if you are not a fool.

[I, 3201]

Every opposite is made evident by its opposite;
honey is perceived as sweet in contrast to vinegar.

[I, 3211]

Anyone not flying to the Lord of Glory
must suppose himself perfect.
There is no worse sickness for the soul,
O you who are proud, than this pretense of perfection.
The heart and eyes must bleed a lot
before self-complacency falls away.

[I, 3213-5]

Can the water of a polluted stream
clear out the dung?
Can human knowledge sweep away
the ignorance of the sensual self?
How does a sword fashion its own hilt?
Go, entrust the cure of this wound to a surgeon,
for flies will gather around the wound
until it can't be seen.
These are your selfish thoughts and all you dream of owning.
The wound is your own dark hole.

[I, 3221-4]

God has made reputation heavy
as a thousand pounds of iron.
So many are bound in that unseen chain!
Pride and lack of faith block
the doorway of repentance
so that the one in separation
can't even utter a sigh.
God said, "*We have put chains around their necks chin high,
and forced them to lift their heads.*"
Those chains aren't put on us from outside.

[I, 3240-2]

Your earthly beloved eclipses
the face of the Divine;
your worldly guide speaks louder
than the words of your true spiritual guide.
Many are the unbelievers who long
for submission,
but their stumbling block
is reputation and pride and continual desires.

[I, 3245-6]

Be cheerful, call for help
to the One who comes at the call,
saying, "Forgive us, You who *love* to forgive."

[I, 3252-3]

O brother, Wisdom is pouring into you
from the beloved saint of God.
You've only borrowed it.
Although the house of your heart
is lit from inside,
that light is lent by a luminous neighbor.
Give thanks; don't be arrogant or vain;
pay attention without self-importance.
It's sad that this borrowed state
has put religious communities
far from religious communion.

[I, 3255-8]

I'm the devoted slave
of anyone who doesn't claim
to have attained dining with God
at every way station.
Many inns must be left behind
before you reach your home.

[I, 3259-61]

A conceited person sees someone sin,
and the flames of Hell rise up in him.
He calls that hellish pride defense of the Religion;
he doesn't notice his own arrogant soul.

[I, 3347-8]

Many people do works of devotion
and set their hearts on approval, expecting rewards.
It's really a hidden sin.
That which the pietist thinks pure
is really foul.

[I, 3384-5]

Everyone is a child
except the one who's intoxicated with God.
No one is an adult
except the one who is free from desire.

[I, 3430]

God has said, *"Like an ass laden with books."*
Knowledge that isn't from Him is a burden.
like a woman's makeup, it doesn't last.
When you carry the burden well,
it will be lifted from you and replaced with spiritual joy.
Beware! Don't carry this burden selfishly.
Control yourself; mount and ride
on the smooth-paced steed of knowledge.
Let the burden fall from your shoulders.

[I, 3448-52]

Be cleansed of the self's features,
and see your pure Self:
behold within your heart all the sciences of the prophets,
without books and without a teacher.

[I, 3460-1]

Know the mirror of the heart is infinite.
Either the understanding falls silent,
or it leads you astray,
because the heart is *with* God,
or indeed the heart *is* He.

[I, 3488-91]

Those with mirror-like hearts
do not depend on fragrance and color:
they behold Beauty in the moment.
They've cracked open the shell of knowledge
and raised the banner
of the eye of certainty.
Thought is gone in a flash of light.

[I, 3492-4]

Everyone is so afraid of death,
but the real sufis just laugh:
nothing tyrannizes their hearts.
What strikes the oyster shell doesn't damage the pearl.

[I, 3495-6]

The body, like a mother,
is pregnant with the spirit-child:
death is the labor of birth.
All the spirits who have passed over
are waiting to see
how that proud spirit shall be born.

[I, 3514-5]

The Prophet said, "When you lay one finger
over an eye, you see the world without the sun.
One fingertip hides the moon—
and this is a symbol of God's covering—
the whole world may be hidden from view
by a single point,
and the sun may be eclipsed by a splinter."
Close your lips and gaze on the sea within you:
God made the sea subject to man.

[I, 3555-8]

Just as your two eyes are under the control of the heart
and subject to the spirit's command,
all five senses move as the heart directs.
Hand and foot also move
like the staff in the hand of Moses.
If the heart wills, at once the foot begins to dance,
from neediness towards abundance.

[I, 3562; 3566-9]

If the heart wills, the hand gathers
the fingers to write a book.
Surely the heart is
the seal of Solomon,
and holds the reins of the senses.
Five external senses are easy for it to manage;
five internal senses are also under its control.
There are ten senses
and seven limbs of the body:
recount to yourself what isn't mentioned here.

[I, 3570; 3575-7]

Whatever it is you wish to marry,
go, absorb yourself in that beloved,
assume its shape and qualities.
If you wish for the light, prepare yourself
to receive it; if you wish to be far from God,
nourish your egoism and drive yourself away.
If you wish to find a way out of this ruined prison,
don't turn your head away from the Beloved,
but *bow in worship and draw near.*

[I, 3605-7]

If the heart is restored to health,
and purged of sensuality,
then *The Merciful God is seated on the Throne.*
After this, He guides the heart directly,
since the heart is with Him.

[I, 3665-6]

Look at yourself, trembling, afraid of non-existence:
know that non-existence
is also afraid
that God might bring it into *existence*.
If you grasp at worldly dignities,
it's from fear, too.
Everything, except love of the Most Beautiful,
is really agony. It's agony
to move towards death and not drink the water of life.

[I, 3684-7]

Fiery lust is not diminished by indulging it,
but inevitably by leaving it ungratified.
As long as you are laying logs on the fire,
the fire will burn.
When you withhold the wood, the fire dies,
and God carries the water.

[I, 3703-6]

Though the worlds are eighteen thousand and more,
not every eye can see them.
Every atom is indeed a place of the vision of God,
but so long as it is unopened,
who says, "There is a door"?

[I, 3756; 3766]

When the time comes for the embryo
to receive the spirit of life,
at that time the sun begins to help.
This embryo is brought into movement,
for the sun quickens it with spirit.

From the other stars this embryo
received only an impression,
until the sun shone upon it.
How did it become connected
with the shining sun
in the womb?

By ways hidden from our senses:
the way whereby gold is nourished,
the way a common stone becomes a garnet
and the ruby red,
the way fruit is ripened,
and the way courage comes
to one distraught
with fear.

[I, 3775-82]

Anger is a king over kings,
but anger once bridled may serve.

[I, 3799]

Night cancels the business of day;
inertia recharges the mind.
Then the day cancels the night,
and inertia disappears in the light.
Though we sleep and rest in the dark,
doesn't the dark contain the water of life?
Be refreshed in the darkness.
Doesn't a moment of silence
restore beauty to the voice?
Opposites manifest through opposites:
in the black core of the heart
God created the eternal light of love.

[I, 3861-65]

He alone has the right to break,
for He alone has the power to mend.
He that knows how to sew together,
knows how to tear apart:
whatever He sells,
He buys something better in exchange.
He lays the house in ruins;
then in a moment He makes it more liveable than before.

[I, 3882-6]

And there is nothing but We have the storehouses thereof,
and We do not send it down but in certain measure.
Without water, earth cannot become a brick,
neither will it become a brick when there is too much water.

[II, Prologue]

A hungry mouth bandages the eyes against the other world:
close this mouth and see clearly.

[II, 11]

The spirit came from God and will return to God.
The present life is only a moment in between.

[II, 12]

If consciousness is paired with another consciousness,
    light increases and the way becomes clear;
        but if a beast joins with another,
    darkness increases and the way disappears.

[II, 26-27]

When the mirror of your heart becomes clear and pure,
    you'll behold images which are outside this world.
      You will see the image and the image-Maker,
        both the carpet of the spiritual expanse
          and the One who spreads it.

[II, 72-3]

The Beautiful attracts the beautiful.
Know this for sure.
Recite the text, *The good women for the good men.*
In this world everything attracts something.
Those of the Fire attract those of the Fire;
those of the Light attract those of the Light.

[II, 80-2]

Many prayers are destructive,
which God in kindness ignores.

[II, 140]

If an artful enemy takes your wealth,
a thief will have robbed a thief.

[II, 134]

Whoever plants thistle in the world,
don't look for him in the rose garden.

[II, 153]

The sufi's book is not of ink and letters;
it is nothing but a heart white as snow.

[II, 159]

The Sun, which is spirit,
became separated into rays through the windows
which are bodies.
When you gaze on the Sun's disk, it is one,
but one who is screened by his perception
of bodies is in some doubt.
Plurality is in the animal spirit;
the human spirit is one essence.
Inasmuch as *God sprinkled his light upon them,*
they are essentially one.
His light never really separated.

[II, 186-9]

Don't make your home in other men's land;
do your own work, don't do the work of a stranger.
Who is the stranger?
Your earth body, the source of all your sorrow.
The hypocrite puts musk on his body
and puts his spirit in the ash-pit.

[II, 263-4; 268]

Don't put musk on your body,
rub it on your heart.
What is musk?
The holy name of the Glorious God.

[II, 267]

If your thought is a rose,
you *are* a rose garden;
if it is a thorn,
you are fuel for the bath stove.

[II, 278]

Though you may learn wisdom by rote,
it leaves when you're unworthy to receive it.
But if you don't read and it sees your ardor of love,
Knowledge will be a docile bird, obedient to your hand.

[II, 318-21]

Prayer and praise were given to you,
but that prayer
made your heart proud.
You thought yourself so intimate with God,
but many became separated from God this way.

[II, 339-40]

You have neglected to give thanks for the Religion
because you got it for nothing from your father.
How should a man who inherits know the value of wealth?

[II, 371-2]

When I cause anyone to weep, My mercy is aroused:
the one with tears drinks of My bounty.
If I don't wish to give,
then I don't show him the gift he desires;
but when I have contracted his heart with grief,
I open it with joy.
My mercy is dependent on that sincere weeping:
when he weeps, waves rise from the sea of My mercy.

[II, 375]

He in whose face the Beloved smiles sweetly,
what harm can befall him
from the sour looks of other people?

[II, 414]

Water doesn't lose purity
because of a bit of weed.
The weeds float on the surface;
the pure water flows on undisturbed.

[II, 418-9]

The Jesus of your spirit is within you:
ask his aid,
for he is a good helper.
Don't seek from your Jesus the comforts of the body.
Don't ask from your Moses the wish of a Pharoah.
Don't burden your heart with thoughts
of livelihood; livelihood will not fail.
Be constant in attendance at the Divine court.

[II, 450; 453-4]

This body is a tent for the spirit,
an ark for Noah.

[II, 455]

You, who have made it easy
for us to labor fruitlessly in the world,
deliver us!
To us it seems a tempting bait,
and it's really a hook:
show it to us as it really is.

[II, 466-7]

Opinions are sometimes wrong,
but what kind of opinion is this
that's blind to the right road?
O eye, you cry for others:
sit down awhile and weep for yourself!
The bough is made green and fresh
by the weeping cloud for the same reason
that the candle is made brighter
by its weeping.

[II, 478-480]

The reflection cast from good friends is needed
until you become, without the aid of any reflector,
a drawer of water from the Sea.
Know that the reflection is at first just imitation,
but when it continues to recur,
it turns into direct realization of truth.
Until it has become realization,
don't part from the friends who guide you—
don't break away from the shell
if the raindrop hasn't yet become a pearl.

[II, 566-8]

Every prophet has said in sincerity,
to his people, "I don't ask wages for my message.
I am only a guide. It is God who purchases:
God has appointed me to act
as broker on both sides."

[II, 573-4]

Patience is crowned with faith:
where one has no patience,
one has no faith.
The Prophet said, "God hasn't given faith to anyone
in whose nature there is no patience."

[II, 600-1]

The world is full of remedies,
but you have no remedies until God
opens a window for you.
Though you are unaware of that remedy now,
God will make it clear
in the hour of need.

[II, 682-3]

Turn back from existence towards non-existence,
if you seek the Lord and belong to the Lord.
Non-existence is the place of income;
don't run away from it.
This existence of more and less
is the place where we spend.

[II, 688-9]

That which is the object of love
is not the form—
whether it is love for the things of this world
or the world beyond.

[II, 703]

Sunlight fell upon the wall;
the wall received a borrowed splendor.
Why set your heart on a piece of earth,
O simple one? Seek out the source
which shines forever.

[II, 708-9]

You who are in love with your intellect—
considering yourself superior to worshippers of form—
that intellect is a beam
of Universal Intellect cast upon your senses;
regard it as gilded gold upon your copper.

[II, 710-11]

Little by little God takes away human beauty:
little by little the sapling withers.
Go, recite *To whomever we give a length of days,
We also cause them to decline.*
Seek the spirit;
don't set your heart on bones.

[II, 714-5]

The beauty of the heart
is the lasting beauty:
its lips give to drink of the water of life.
Truly it is the water, that which pours,
and the one who drinks—all three
become one when your talisman is shattered.
That oneness you can't know by reasoning.

[II, 716-8]

On the back of the donkey
are the goods and the money;
but the pearl of your heart
is the investment which supports
a hundred donkeys.

[II, 726]

The ass, your fleshly soul,
has wandered off; tie it down.
How long will it run away from work?
Let it bear the burden of patience
and gratitude—whether for a hundred years,
or for thirty or twenty.

[II, 729-30]

The discovery of treasure is by luck,
and even more, it is rare:
one must earn a living
so long as the body is able.
Does earning a livelihood
prevent the discovery of treasure?
Don't retire from work:
that treasure, indeed,
follows after the work.

[II, 734-5]

A certain stranger was hastily seeking a home,
　　so a friend took him to a house in ruins.
　　　"If this house had a roof," he said,
　　　　"you could live next to me.
　　Your family would be comfortable here, too,
　　　　if there were another room."
"Yes," he said, "it's nice to be next door to friends,
　　but my dear soul, one cannot lodge in 'if'."

[II, 739-42]

If you have a touchstone, go ahead, choose;
otherwise, go and devote yourself
to one who knows the differences.
Either you must have a touchstone
within your own soul,
or if you don't know the way,
find someone who does.

[II, 746-7]

The Worker is hidden in the workshop:
enter the workshop if you want to see Him.
Since the workshop is where He is,
the one outside is unaware of Him.
So come into the workshop—that is to say,
non-existence—and see
the work together with the Worker.

[II, 759; 761-2]

Envy makes you say, "I'm inferior
to so and so: and his good luck
increases *my* lack."
Indeed envy is a defect;
worse than any other.

[II, 805]

Inasmuch as no one was ever disgraced
by inferiority to God,
no one has ever been envious of God.

[II, 812]

The fire that iron or gold need—
would it be good for fresh quinces and apples?
The apple and quince are just slightly raw;
unlike iron, they need only a gentle heat.
But gentle flames are not enough for iron;
it eagerly draws to itself the fiery dragon's breath.
That iron is the dervish who bears hardship:
under the hammer and fire, he happily glows red.

[II, 827-30]

If the heart isn't there,
how can the body speak?
If the heart doesn't seek,
how then can the body seek?

[II, 837]

Man is concealed beneath his tongue;
this tongue is the curtain over the door of the soul.
When a gust of wind has pushed aside the curtain,
the secret of the interior of the house is disclosed.
We see whether in that house there are pearls
or grains of wheat, a treasure of gold,
or all scorpions and snakes; or whether a treasure
is there and a serpent beside it,
since a treasure of gold is never
without someone to keep watch.

[II, 846-8]

If your knowledge of fire has been turned
to certainty by words alone,
then seek to be cooked by the fire itself.
Don't abide in borrowed certainty.
There is no real certainty until you burn;
if you wish for this, sit down in the fire.

[II, 860-1]

When the ear is penetrating, it becomes an eye.
Otherwise, the word of God becomes entangled
in the ear and does not reach the heart.

[II, 862]

It's not necessary to burn a new blanket
on account of a flea;
nor would I turn my back
on you because of superficial faults.

[II, 871]

Anyone who sees their own faults
before noticing those of others,
why don't they correct themselves?
People of the world don't look at themselves,
and so they blame one another.

[II, 880-1]

On the bank of the river,
water is grudged by that one alone
who is blind to the flowing stream.

[II, 894]

Stinginess is not seeing the abundance:
the prospect of pearls keeps the diver glad.

[II, 898]

Generosity, then, comes from the eye—
not from the hand—it's seeing that matters:
only one who sees is saved.

[II, 900]

God did not need the prophets,
but with majesty and grace
let His lightning Beauty strike.
Adam received from that light
his knowledge of God.
With that radiance
Abraham went fearlessly
into the fire.

[II 906; 910; 913]

What do you really possess,
and what have you gained?
What pearls have you brought up
from the depth of the sea?
On the day of death,
bodily senses will vanish:
do you have the spiritual light
to accompany your heart?
When dust fills these eyes in the grave,
will your grave shine bright?

[II, 939-41]

The fruits are first in our thoughts,
but only in the end
are they truly seen.
When you have done the work
and planted the tree,
when the fruit appears,
you read the first words.

[II, 971-2]

You can't sit inactive for a moment;
you can't rest until some good or bad
has come out of you.
These impulses to action
bring your inner consciousness
more clearly into outer view.
How then should the reel-
which is the body—
become still, when the line's end—
which is the mind—is pulling.

[II, 996-8]

This world and that world are forever giving birth:
every cause is a mother; the effect born is as a child.
When the effect was born, it too became a cause,
so that it might give birth to wondrous effects.
These causes follow generation upon generation,
but it takes a very well-illumined eye
to see all the links in the chain.

[II, 1000-2]

Know that the outward form passes away,
but the world of reality remains forever.
How long will you play at loving the shape of the jug?
Leave the jug; go, seek the water!

[II, 1020-1]

These shells of bodies in the world,
　　　　though they are all living
　　　by grace of the Sea of the Soul—
yet there isn't a pearl in every shell.
　　　Open your eyes and look
　　　into the heart of each one.
Find out what is within each one,
for that costly pearl is rarely found.

[II, 1023-5]

By a single thought that comes into the mind,
in one moment a hundred worlds are overturned.

[II, 1029]

When you see that from a thought
every craft in the world arises and subsists—
that houses and palaces and cities,
mountains and plains and rivers,
earth and ocean as well as sun and sky,
derive their life from it as fish from the sea—
then why in your foolishness, O blind one,
does the body seem to you a Solomon,
and thought only as an ant?

[II, 1034-7]

You think the shadow is the substance:
so to you the *substance* has become a cheap toy.
Wait until the day when that substance
freely unfolds its wings.
Then you will see the mountains become as soft as wool,
and this earth of heat and ice become as nothing;
you will see neither the sky nor the stars,
nor any existence but God—the One, the Living, the Loving.

[II, 1042-5]

The melodies of David were so dear
to the faithful, but to the faithless
they were no more than the noise of wood.

[II, 1074]

Man's original food is the light of God;
material food is not for him;
but from disease,
his mind has fallen into the delusion
that day and night he should eat only this food.
He is pale, weak, and faint:
where is the food of *by heaven*
which has starry tracks?
That is the food of the chosen,
food eaten without fork or throat.

[II, 1083-6]

The heart eats a particular food from every companion;
the heart receives a particular nourishment
from every single piece of knowledge.

[II, 1089]

Just as the heart becomes carefree
in a place of green, growing plants,
goodwill and kindness are born
when our souls enter happiness.

[II, 1095-6]

The false self can become just dust,
dust in which only His footprints remain.
Become dust for His footprints,
and one day you will be His crown.

[II, 1175]

The Universal Soul met a separate soul
and placed a pearl on her breast.
Through such contact the soul, like Mary,
became pregnant with a heart-winning messiah.

[II, 1183-4]

These sayings of mine are really a call to God,
   words to lure the breath of that sweet One.
How can you be silent? How can you fail to call,
   knowing He always answers, "Here I am—"
   that silent answer you feel from head to toe.

[II, 1189-91]

The more anyone loves the sound of invisible waters,
   the more he tears bricks from the wall
to toss into that unseen river, drunk with that sound
   which the loveless hear as just a splash.

[II, 1213-4]

Know that every bad habit is a thornbush.
After all, how often have you stepped on its thorns?

[II, 1240]

Either take up your axe and strike
like Ali at the gates of Khaybar.*
Or join these thorns with a rose:
bring your fire to God's light in order that
your fire will disappear in His light,
and all your thorns become roses.

[II, 1244-6]

* Khaybar: A heavily fortified city in Arabia.

The faithful one is a fountain of mercy:
the pure spirit of the well-doer is the water of life.

[II, 1253]

The worm is in the root of the body's tree;
it must be dug out and burned.
Travelers, it is late.
Life's sun is going to set.
During these brief days that you have strength,
be quick and spare no effort of your wings.

[II, 1264-6]

The sensuous eye is a horse;
the light of God is the rider:
without the rider the horse is useless.
The light of God rides the body's eye.
The soul yearns for God.
God's light enhances the senses.
This is the meaning of *Light upon Light.*

[II, 1286, 1290-3]

See how the hand is invisible while the pen is writing;
the horse careening, yet the rider unseen;
the arrow flying, but the bow out of sight;
individual souls existing,
while the Soul of souls is hidden.

[II, 1303-4]

Break your anger, not the arrow:
the eye of anger sees milk as blood.
Give the arrow a kiss and bring it to the King,
the arrow stained with your own blood.

[II, 1307-8]

No mirror ever became iron again;
no bread ever became wheat;
no ripened grape ever became sour fruit.
Mature yourself and be secure
from a change for the worse. Become the Light.

[II, 1317-8]

The shaikh, like God,
works without tools,
teaches without words.

[II, 1323]

Whose voice echoes in the mountains of the heart?
Sometimes the mountains are filled with it,
and sometimes empty.
Wherever He is, He is the master.
May His voice never abandon these mountains.

[II, 1327-8]

The baptism of God is the dyeing vat of *Hu*,
God's absoluteness, in which all colors become one.
When the contemplative falls into that vat—
and you say, "Come out."
He says, "I am the vat. Don't blame me."
That "I am the vat,"
means the same as "I am God."
The red-hot iron has taken on the color of fire.

[II, 1345-7]

Sometimes it is better to be with a disrespectful person
than to be alone.
Even if the handle is damaged,
at least it is attached to a door.

[II, 1360]

Water says to the dirty, "Come here."
The dirty one says, "I'm so ashamed."
Water says, "How will your shame be washed away
without me?"

[II, 1366-7]

The ocean of the body crashes
against the ocean of the heart.
Between them is *a barrier they cannot cross.*

[II, 1371]

My soul is a furnace
happy with the fire.
Love, too, is a furnace,
and ego its fuel.

[II, 1376-7]

When the pain of love increases your joy,
roses and lilies fill the garden of your soul.

[II, 1379]

Every link of the chain is a different madness
and every moment is a different link.

[II, 1382-3]

Within the human being is a jungle.
You, born of the Divine Breath, be aware.
Wolves and pigs by the thousands are within,
the fair and the foul.
What dominates within is what you are.
If your gold outweighs your copper,
you will be known as gold. Whatever you most are
is the form in which you will resurrect.

[II, 1416-9]

How will you know your real friends?
Pain is as dear to them as life.
A friend is like gold. Trouble is like fire.
Pure gold delights in the fire.

[II, 1458; 1461]

Regard as a king someone unconcerned with kingship.
Only he who is an enemy to his own existence
possesses real existence.

[II, 1469-70]

No matter what plans you make,
no matter what you acquire,
the thief will enter from the unguarded side.
Be occupied, then, with what you really value
and let the thief take something less.

[II, 1505-7]

141

By love, the bitter becomes sweet;
by love, copper becomes gold;
by love, the dregs become clear;
by love, the dead become living;
by love, the king becomes a slave.
From knowledge, love grows.
Has stupidity ever placed someone on such a throne?

[II, 1529-32]

Lightning is quick and unpredictable.
Only with a clear mind will you know
the transient from the stable.
Lightning laughs at those who would capture its light.

[II, 1542-3]

It is the nature of Reason to see to the End;
  it is the nature of desire not to.

[II, 1548]

God turns you from one feeling to another
  and teaches by means of opposites,
  so that you will have two wings to fly,
  not one.

[II, 1552; 1554]

Is there a window from heart to heart?
After all, the shaikh sees your thoughts
  as if through a window.

[II, 1587]

Beware! Don't allow yourself to do
what you know is wrong, relying on the thought,
"Later I will repent and ask God's forgiveness."
True repentence flashes inside and rains tears.
Such lightning and clouds are needed.
Without the lightning of the heart
and the rain storms of the eyes,
how shall the fire of Divine wrath be calmed?
How shall the greenery grow
and fountains of clear water pour forth?

[II, 1652-56]

As far as you can, do not set foot in separation.
God has said, "Of all the things allowed
the most hateful to Me is divorce."

[II, 1752]

For God's lovers, blood is better than water.
The mistake of a lover is better
than a hundred proper actions of anyone else.

[II, 1767]

The religion of Love is like no other.
For lovers, the only religion and belief is God.

[II, 1770]

Do not seek any rules or method of worship.
Say whatever your pained heart chooses.

[II, 1784]

The breath of the flute player,
does it belong to the flute?

[II, 1793]

The unsuspecting child first wipes the tablet
and then writes the letters on it.
God turns the heart into blood and desperate tears;
then He writes the spiritual mysteries on it.

[II, 1826-7]

The porter runs to the heavy load and takes it from others,
  knowing burdens are the foundation of ease
  and bitter things the forerunners of pleasure.
    See the porters struggle over the load!
  It's the way of those who see the truth of things.

[II, 1834-6]

Paradise is surrounded by what we dislike;
the fires of hell are surrounded by what we desire.

[II, 1837]

Have pity on Jesus, but not on the donkey:
don't allow your animal nature to rule your reason.
Let it weep bitterly; take from it
what you need to pay your debt.
For years you have been the donkey's slave. Enough!

[II, 1853-5]

In Jesus reason was strong, and the donkey was weak.
The donkey is made lean by a strong rider.
But often from the weakness of reason,
this worn-out ass has become a dragon.

[II, 1859-60]

Unkindness from the wise
is better than the kindness of the ignorant.
The Prophet said, "Enmity from wisdom
is better than love which comes from a fool."

[II, 1876-7]

The ass runs from his master because it's assinine;
the master runs after the ass out of good will.
He seeks him, not from profit or loss,
but so that the wolf will not tear him to pieces.

[II, 1899-1900]

Lovingkindness is drawn to the saint, as medicine goes
to the pain it must cure.
Where there is pain, the remedy follows:
wherever the lowlands are, the water goes.
If you want the water of mercy, make yourself low;
then drink the wine of mercy and be drunk.
Mercy upon mercy rises to your head like a flood.
Don't settle on a single mercy, O son.
Bring the sky beneath your feet
and listen to celestial music everywhere.

[II, 1938-42]

Tear the shackle, which is the body,
from the feet of your soul,
so that you can race around the arena.
Loosen the bonds of avarice from your hands and neck:
seize and enjoy a new wealth in the old heaven.

[II, 1948-9]

When you have seen your own cunning,
follow it back to its origin.
What is below comes from above.
Come on, turn your eyes to the heights.

[II, 1973-4]

Looking up gives light,
though at first it makes you dizzy.
Get used to this light, unless you're a bat.
The sign of your having this light
is your vision of the end.
The lust of the moment is in truth your dark grave.

[II, 1975-7]

Many talents run through your head
that urge you to fame.
The truth is that
your head will be lost.
If you don't wish to lose your head,
make yourself lowly like a foot.
Put yourself under the protection
of the axis who has discernment.

[II, 1983-4]

O God, make our stony hearts soft as wax;
make our wailing sweet and the object of Your mercy.

[II, 1992]

We would hide the truth from
the sorrowful one, whose bowl
has fallen from the roof,*
but it can't be hid.
While that ignorant one—
that stranger to love's sorrow,
to whom truth has been shown
so many times—cannot see it.
The mirror of the heart must be clear,
so you may know the ugly from the beautiful.

[II, 2061-3]

* An idiom describing one who has fallen into ecstasy.

When the remedy you have offered
only increases the disease,
then leave him who will not be cured,
and tell your story
to someone who seeks the truth.

[II, 2067]

Remember the adage: Men are mines.
One mine may be worth a hundred thousand.
One mine of lurking ruby and carnelian
has more value than countless mines of copper.
O Ahmad, here riches are of no use!
What is wanted is a heart full of love and pain and sighs.

[II, 2077-9]

The unbeliever supposes he has hurt me;
but no, he has wiped the dust from my mirror.

[II, 2094]

When two people have come into touch with each other,
without any doubt, they have something in common.
How should a bird fly except with its own kind?

[II, 2101-2]

The garden is the home of the nightingale;
the dung heap is suitable to the beetle.

[II, 2116]

You may despair of finding a true friend of God;
but since the treasure does exist in this world,
consider no ruin empty of treasure.
Go to every dervish at random,
and when you find the sign of a true saint,
keep his company regularly.
If the inner eye has not been granted to you,
always think that treasure could be in anybody.

[II, 2153-5]

Whoever wants to sit with God,
let him sit in the presence of the saints.

[II, 2163]

If gossip tears a friend away from you,
don't patiently suffer the separation.

[II, 2180]

Many wonders are manifest in sleep:
in sleep the heart becomes a window.
One that is awake and dreams beautiful dreams,
he is the knower of God. Receive the dust of his eyes.

[II, 2235-6]

Pain is a treasure of mercy:
the fruit is juicy when you peel the rind.

[II, 2261]

Conventional opinion is the ruin of our souls,
something borrowed which we mistake as our own.
Ignorance is better than this; clutch at madness instead.
Always run from what seems to benefit your self:
sip the poison and spill the water of life.
Revile those who flatter you;
lend both interest and principal to the poor.
Let security go and be at home amid dangers.
Leave your good name behind and accept disgrace.
I have lived with cautious thinking;
now I'll make myself mad.

[II, 2327-32]

If a saint wears a veil of madness,
will you who are blind recognize him?
But, if your intuitive eye is open,
behold a commander under every stone.

[II, 2346-7]

Knowledge is conventional and borrowed
when its owner is annoyed
by people who aren't fascinated by it.
Since it was learned as a bait for popularity,
and not for enlightenment,
the seeker of religious knowledge
is no better than the seeker of worldly knowledge.
He seeks to please the vulgar and noble,
rather than to attain freedom from this world.
Like a mouse he has burrowed in every direction;
afraid of the light, he prefers to work in darkness.

[II, 2429-35]

Dialectical knowledge, which is soulless,
    enjoys the faces of its customers—
       full of energy in the dispute,
but dead and gone when there is no customer.
    My customer is God: He lifts me up,
       for *God has purchased.*

[II, 2436-8]

O Lord, truly, Your grace is not from our work,
    but from Your mysterious giving.
Save us from what our own hands might do;
    lift the veil, but do not tear it.
Save us from the ego; its knife has reached our bones.
    Who but You will break these chains?
    Let us turn from ourselves to You
    Who are nearer to us than ourselves.
    Even this prayer is Your gift to us.
How else has a rose garden grown from these ashes?

[II, 2443-9]

Through the window between heart and heart
flashes the light that tells truth from lie.

[II, 2462]

Delusion is a Divine curse
that makes someone envious, conceited, malicious,
so that he doesn't know the evil he does
will strike him back.
If he could see his nothingness
and his deadly, festering wound,
pain would arise from looking within,
and that pain would save him.

[II, 2513-7]

To say you have no pain is like saying, "I am God."
    To say "I" at the wrong time is a curse.
    To say "I" at the right time is a gift of God.
    For Hallaj it was timely; for Pharoah a lie.
    Behead the rooster that crows too early.

[II, 2521-4]

The faithful bow willingly,
    intending the pleasure of God.
The unbeliever worships God, but unwillingly,
    intending some other desire.
Yes, he keeps the King's fortress in good repair,
    but claims to be in command.

[II, 2544-6]

One who sees without distortion, free of prejudice,
has light in the eyes.
Self-interest blinds you
and buries your knowledge in a grave.
Lack of prejudice makes ignorance wise;
its presence makes knowledge perverse.
Accept no bribe, and your sight is clear;
act selfishly, and you become blind and enslaved.

[II, 2550-3]

In this world you have become clothed and rich,
but when you come out of this world, how will you be?
Learn a trade that will earn you forgiveness.
In the world beyond there's also traffic and trade.
Beside those earnings, this world is just play.
As children embrace in fantasy intercourse,
or set up a candy shop, this world is a game.
Night falls, and the child
comes home hungry, without his friends.

[II, 2593-9]

Iblis asked, "Can you tell a lie from the truth,
    you who are filled with illusion?"
Muawiya answered, "The Prophet has given a clue,
    a touchstone to know
    the base coin from the true.
He has said, 'That which is false troubles the heart,
    but Truth brings joyous tranquility.'"

[II, 2732-4]

The troubled heart finds no comfort in lies:
    water and oil kindle no light.
Only truthful speech brings comfort:
    truths are the bait that attract the heart.

[II, 2735-6]

When the heart becomes whole,
it will know the flavors of falsehood and truth.
When Adam's greed for the forbidden fruit increased,
it robbed his heart of health.
Discernment flies
from one who is drunken with desire.
He who puts down that cup
lightens the inner eye,
and the secret is revealed.

[II, 2738-43]

Everyone who delights in some act of devotion
can't bear to miss it,
even for a short while.
That disappointment and grief
are as a hundred prayers:
what is ritual prayer compared
with the glow of humble longing?

[II, 2769-70]

In union with God, of what value are signs?
The one who is blind to Essence
sees Divine action through the attributes:
having lost the Essence he is limited to evidences.
Those who are united with God
are absorbed in the Essence.
How should they focus on His qualities?
When your head is submerged in the sea,
how will your eye fall on the color of the water?

[II, 2811-4]

When you are called into His presence,
and then driven back to the threshold,
know it is your own doing, for sure.
It is foolishness to claim you were compelled,
saying, "This is my predestined lot."
Why were you lucky yesterday?
You yourself have blocked the giving.
The worthy augment their lot.

[II, 2821-4]

Courtesy that comes to the tongue
without sincerity of the heart and soul
is like herbs on the ash heap, O friends.
Look at that greenery from a distance and pass by:
it isn't fit to eat or even smell.

[II, 2840-1]

Broken promises are the result of stupidity;
faithfulness to one's word is the practice
of one who fears God with love.

[II, 2875]

If you scrutinize the labor of those who follow falsehood,
you'll see that it stinks—
layer upon layer, like an onion—
every effort more pithless than the next.
While with the sincere,
every effort is finer than the one before.

[II, 2900-1]

Nothing shows up false without the true:
the fool took false coin
hoping it might be gold.
If there were no genuine coin in the world,
how would it be possible to pass fakes?
Unless there is truth,
how could there be lies?
Falsity gets its value from the existence of truth.
Some want the wrong in hope that it will be right.

[II, 2928-2931]

Truth is the Night of Power,
hidden amid the other nights
so the soul may try each one.
Not all nights are the Night of Power,
yet all nights aren't empty of it either.

[II, 2935-6]

If not for the faulty things in the world,
every fool would be a shrewd merchant.
Then it would be easy to know the value of goods.

[II, 2939-40]

The sky, so beautiful and glorious:
God said, "*Then turn thy gaze again towards it.*"
As regards this roof of light,
don't be content with just one look:
look many times; see:
Are there any flaws?
Since He has told you to look often
at this excellent roof, examining it for flaws,
know then, how much discernment the dark earth needs.

[II, 2946-9]

The difficulties of winter and autumn,
the heat of summer,
spring like the spirit of life,
winds and clouds and lightning—all these
help to make distinctions clear:
so the dust-colored earth
may bring forth all it holds in its heart,
whether ruby or dull stone.

[II, 2951-3]

The High God lays upon our body, O lion-hearted,
heat and cold and grief and pain,
fear and hunger and poverty and illness—
all for the soul—
so the soul's true coin may be seen and used.

[II, 2963-4]

Give him milk, mother of Moses,
   then cast him into the water.
Don't be afraid of putting him to the test.
Whoever drank that milk in pre-eternity
   distinguishes the true milk here,
just as Moses knew his own mother's milk.

[II, 2969-70]

Be warm, you who are cool, that heat may come;
   bear difficulties, that ease may come.

[II, 3011]

Expression always falls short of meaning.
The Prophet said, "Whoever knows God, his tongue falters."
Speech is an astrolabe in its reckoning.
How much does it really know of the sky and the sun?
Or of that Sky which holds this heaven as a speck;
and that Sun which shows this sun to be a grain of sand?

[II, 3013-5]

When it comes to human essences,
the foundation of these buildings we build,
know there are differences.
Neither is one person's life like another,
nor is any death the same.
Never think anyone's grave is similar.
How indeed shall I describe the difference that exists
among souls in that other world?
Put your work to the touchstone as you work.

[II, 3022-5]

O, happy the soul that saw its own faults,
and if anyone mentioned a fault,
wished eagerly to take responsibility—
for half of each person
has always belonged to the realm of fault,
but the other half belongs
to the Realm of the Unseen.

[II, 3034-5]

Since you have ten sores on your head,
you must apply the medicine to yourself.
Recognizing your own illness is the right remedy;
when you repent and are humbled,
it is then the right time
to obey the Prophet's command,
"Have mercy."

[II, 3036-7]

Even if you don't have the same fault as another,
don't be secure;
maybe later that fault will be yours.
For years Iblis lived in good favor,
yet in the end disgrace enveloped him:
mark well the meaning of his name.
Satan's soul was tried by the wrath of God;
he stumbled;
and in his fall became a warning to you.
He drank the poison:
eat the sugar!

[II, 3038-45]

Someone says, "I can't help feeding my family.
I have to work so hard to earn a living."
He can do without God, but not without food;
he can do without Religion,
but not without idols.
Where is one who'll say,
"If I eat bread without awareness of God,
I will choke."

[II, 3071-79]

Anything you can think of is likely to pass away;
but he who doesn't enter into thought is God.

[II, 3107]

Fools honor the mosque
yet seek to destroy those in whose heart God lives.
That mosque is of the world of things;
this heart is real.
The true mosque is nothing but the heart
of spiritual kings.
The mosque that is the inner awareness of the saints
is the place of worship for all:
God is there.

[II, 3108-11]

Come, arise from the depths of your heart!
You are alive and born of the living.
O lovely one, aren't you suffocated
by this narrow tomb?
You are the Joseph of the time, the bright sun:
arise from this prison and show your face!
Your Jonah has been cooked and absorbed
in the belly of the fish:
to deliver him there is no way
but glorification of God.

[II, 3132-5]

This world is a sea, and the body a fish,
and the spirit is Jonah
kept from the light of the dawn.
If the spirit is filled with glorifying God,
it will be delivered from the fish;
otherwise it is digested and disappears.

[II, 3140-1]

To practice patience is the soul of praise:
have patience,
for that is true glorification.
No glorification is worth as much.
Have patience:
patience is the remedy for pain.

[II, 3146]

If you put on the armor of a warrior,
yet are unable to defend yourself, you'll die.
Make your soul a shield,
bear what God sends you,
put down the sword.
Whoever is headless saves his head;
the selfless cannot be struck.
Those weapons are your selfish strategy;
a defense that wounds your own soul.

[II, 3169-71]

If you wish your misery to end,
seek also to lose your wisdom—
the wisdom born of human illusion,
that which lacks the light
of God's overflowing grace.
The wisdom of this world increases doubt;
the wisdom of Faith releases you into the sky.

[II, 3200-3]

Students of cunning have consumed their hearts
and learned only tricks;
They've thrown away real riches:
patience, self-sacrifice, generosity.
Right thought opens a way.

[II, 3205-8]

You're all mixed up.
For the sake of position,
you come with reverence before the blind
and wait in the hall;
but in the presence of those who can see,
you behave with disrespect.
No wonder you've become fuel for the fire of desire.

[II, 3221-2]

If you aren't headed briskly
towards that garden,
then get rid of your congestion
and smell the fragrance.
Let it draw your soul to the garden.

[II, 3232-3]

The five spiritual senses are all connected.
They've grown from one root.
As one grows strong, the others strengthen, too:
each one becomes a cupbearer to the rest.
Seeing with the eye increases speech;
speech increases discernment in the eye.
As sight deepens, it awakens every sense,
so that perception of the spiritual
becomes familiar to them all.

[II, 3236-9]

When one sense grows into freedom,
all the other senses change as well.
When one sense perceives the hidden,
the invisible world becomes apparent to the whole.

[II, 3240-1]

When one sheep of the flock jumps over a stream,
they all jump across on each other's heels.
Drive the sheep, your senses, to pasture:
Let them feed on the pasture shown by
He who has brought forth the herbage,
that they may graze on hyacinth and wild-rose;
and be led to the green meadows of the Realities;
that every one of their senses
may become a prophet to the others,
and lead all senses into that paradise.

[II, 3242-5]

When a dispute arises
as to the ownership of the husk,
the husk belongs
to the one who possesses the kernel.
The heavenly sphere is the husk;
the light of the spirit is the core.
This sky is visible; spirit is not;
but don't stumble because of this.
The body is manifest;
Life's spirit is hidden:
the body is like a sleeve;
the spirit is the hand.

[II, 3251-2]

Sometimes the intellectual thinks
someone filled with spirit acts crazily;
sometimes he is quite bewildered,
since to understand,
he must become spiritual himself.

[II, 3261]

Conventional knowledge is for sale;
when it finds a purchaser,
it glows with delight.
The purchaser of real knowledge is God:
its market is always splendid.
The owner of real knowledge has closed his lips
and is enraptured in his trading:
the buying is without end,
for *God has purchased*.

[II, 3265-7]

The mouse-soul is nothing but a nibbler.
To the mouse is given a mind proportionate to its need,
for without need, the Almighty God
doesn't give anything to anyone.
Need, then, is the net for all things that exist:
man has tools in proportion to his need.
So, quickly, increase your need, needy one,
that the sea of abundance may surge up in lovingkindness.

[II, 3279-80; 3292]

The word is like the nest,
and meaning is the bird:
the body is the riverbed,
and spirit, the rolling water.

[II, 3293]

The surface of thought's stream
carries sticks and straws—
some pleasant, some unsightly.
Seed-husks floating in the water
have fallen from fruits of the invisible garden.
Look for the kernels back in the garden,
for the water comes from the garden into the riverbed.
If you don't see the flow of the water of Life,
look at this movement of weeds in thought's stream.
When the water flows more fully,
the husks, our ideas, pass along more quickly.
When this stream has become a torrent,
no care lingers in the mind of gnostics:
since the water has become so swift and full,
there is no longer room in it for anything but water.

[II, 3296-3302]

The animal soul is Nimrod;
the intellect and spirit are Abraham, the friend of God.
The spirit is concerned with reality itself,
the ego with the proofs.
These signposts on the way
are for the traveler who at every moment
becomes lost in the desert.

[II, 3311-2]

For a newborn child, the father babbles,
though his own intelligence encompasses the world.
One must adopt the child's language
to convey knowledge.
All the people, then, are children to the guide:
this the pir remembers
when he attempts to teach.

[II, 3315; 3317-8]

Before the Infinite,
all that is finite is nothingness:
Everything is passing away,
except the face of God.

[II, 3321]

Spiritual life is knowledge in the time of trial:
the more knowledge you have,
the more spiritual life is yours.
Our spirit is more than animal spirit. How?
It has more knowledge.
The spirit of angels is greater than ours;
it transcends common sense.
Yet the spirit of mystics is greater still.
Don't be bewildered by this.

[II, 3326-9]

What is evil?
The needy, base metal.
Who is the shaikh?
The infinite elixir.
Though the copper proves untransmutable,
still the elixir never becomes copper.
What is evil? A fiery rebel.
Who is the shaikh? The sea of eternity.
Fire is always afraid of water,
but when did water ever fear being set aflame?

[II, 3343-6]

A fine delight is needed for devotions to bear fruit:
a kernel is required for a berry to produce a tree.

[II, 3396]

If sunlight falls upon filth,
still it's the same light:
no contamination comes to it.

[II, 3411]

The Prophet said,"Know that God
makes impure things pure for the spiritually great."*

[II, 3427]

*"On that account the Grace of God has made my place of worship to be pure
everywhere even up to the seventh Heaven." --when his wife Aisha
commented that he prayed anywhere and without a prayer carpet.

Be a servant since you are not a lord:
   don't steer the boat yourself
   since you're not a boatman.

[II, 3454]

Since you're not spiritually perfect,
   don't open a shop on your own.
   Be pliant to the hand,
so you may become leavened and kneaded like dough.
   Listen to the Divine command, "Keep silence."
      Be mute.
Since you haven't become the tongue of God,
      be an ear.
   If you do speak,
   let it be to ask for explanations:
   speak as a humble beggar
   at the hand of the spiritually great.

[II, 3455-7]

The beginning of pride and hatred
lies in worldly desire,
and the strength of your desire is from habit.
When an evil tendency becomes confirmed by habit,
rage is triggered when anyone restrains you.

[II, 3466-7]

Kill the snake of desire in the beginning;
or watch out: your snake will become a dragon.
But everyone considers his own snake to be just an ant:
if you do, seek knowledge of your real state
from one who is a lord of the heart.
Until copper becomes gold,
it doesn't know that it's copper:
until the heart becomes a king,
it doesn't recognize it's poverty.

[II, 3472-4]

Serve the elixir, like copper:
endure oppression, O heart,
from the one who holds the deed.
Who is it who holds the deed to the heart?
Know well, it is the lords of the heart
who, like day and night,
recoil from the world.

[II, 3475-6]

Dervishhood is not for the sake of avoiding
entanglement with the world;
no, it's because nothing exists but God.

[II, 3497]

The lower self philosophizes:
    beat it for its own good,
    arguing with it doesn't help.
It witnesses a prophet's miracle
    and momentarily glows with belief;
but later on says, "That was just imagination;
    for if that incredible sight had been real,
it would have lasted—it would remain before my eyes."
    It is lasting in the eyes of the pure,
    but it doesn't haunt the eyes of animals.
Miracles keep their distance from bodily senses:
    would a peacock stay in a ditch?

[II, 3500-04]

Don't exceed in any quality
the one who shares your yoke,
for certainly separation will follow.

[II, 3514]

Those who wear clothes look to the launderer,
but the naked soul wears illumination.
Either withdraw from the naked
or take off your clothes like them.
If you can't become wholly naked,
take the middle way
and take off at least some
of what you wear.

[II, 3524-5]

Although the middle path is the way of wisdom,
still the middle path is relative.
To a camel, the water in a stream isn't much,
but to a mouse, it is an ocean.
If someone is hungry for four loaves
and eats only two or three, that's moderation;
but if he eats all four, it's far from the mean:
he's bound by greed like a duck.
If someone has hunger for ten loaves and eats six,
that is moderation.
When I have an appetite for fifty loaves,
and you only want six scones,
we aren't equal.

[II, 3531-6]

You may be tired by ten cycles of prayer;
I may not be worn out by five hundred.
One goes barefoot all the way to the Kaa'ba,
and another is totally exhausted
just going as far as the mosque.
One in utter self-devotion gives away his life,
while another agonizes over the gift of a loaf.
This middle way belongs to the realm of the finite,
for that finite has a beginning and end.
A beginning and end are necessary
to conceive of the middle point.
As the Infinite doesn't have limits,
how can you apply a mean to it?

[II, 3537-42]

No one has shown the beginning or end of the Infinite.
God said, *"If the sea were to become ink . . ."*
Still God's word could not be written out.
Though all the orchards and forests were pens,
still we would be no closer to defining it.
Ink and pens pass away,
yet this infinite Word is everlasting.

[II, 3542-6]

The Prophet said, "My eyes sleep,
but my heart is not asleep to the Lord of created beings."
Your eyes are awake,
and your heart is sunk in slumber;
my eyes are asleep,
but my heart is contemplating the opening
of the door of Divine grace.
My heart has five other senses than the physical:
both worlds are the theatre
for the senses of the heart.

[II, 3549-51]

Everyone is overridden by thoughts;
that's why they have so much heartache and sorrow.
At times I give myself up to thought purposefully;
but when I choose,
I spring up from those under its sway.
I am like a high-flying bird,
and thought is a gnat:
how should a gnat overpower me?

[II, 3559-61]

When pure lawful food turns foul in your belly,
put a lock on your throat and hide the key.
Yet anyone in whom food becomes the light
of spiritual glory, let him eat what he will,
it's lawful food for him.

[II, 3571-2]

If you are my soul's familiar friend,
my words of reality
aren't mere remarks.
If at midnight I say,"I am near:
come now don't be afraid of the night,
I am your kin,"
these two assertions are real to you,
since you recognize your own relative's voice;
and even more, your delight
at hearing the voice of your kinsman bears witness
to the truthful presence of your dear friend.

[II; 3573-5, 3578]

Since wisdom is the stray camel of the faithful believer,
he knows it with certainty from whomever he hears it.
When he finds himself right in front of it,
how should he have any doubt?
How should he mistake himself?

[II, 3591-2]

When God gives spiritual awareness to any community,
the face and voice of a prophet
become a miraculous proof.
The prophet calls aloud
and the soul of the community
falls to worship within.
Never had the soul's ear
heard a cry like this.
That stranger, the soul,
immediately perceiving the wondrous voice,
hears from God's own tongue the words,
"Truly, I am near."

[II, 3598-3601]

201

Let the skeptic know:
all that is absent in the world
is present to one who receives ideas from God.
To Mary, John the Baptist's mother would appear,
though she was far away from her.
You can see a friend even with your eyes shut,
when you've made the skin a window for spiritual ideas.

[II, 3612-4]

God said, "Truly there has never been a people
lacking a friend of God,"
someone with power of the spirit;
and he it is who makes the soul-birds sing
unanimously, sincerely,
free of all ill-will.
They become as kind as a mother:
Muhammed said of the Muslims,
"They are like one soul."
Through the Messenger of God they became one;
otherwise they were all enemies absolutely.

[II, 3709-12]

A brotherhood is as a cluster of grapes:
when you squeeze them they become one juice.
The unripe and the ripe are in opposition,
but when the immature ripens, too,
it becomes a good friend.

[II, 3717-8]

The hearty unripe grapes, capable of ripening,
at last become one in heart
by the breath of the masters of heart.
They grow rapidly to grapehood,
shedding duality and hatred and strife.
Then in maturity, they rend their skins,
till they become one:
unity is the proper attribute
for one who is one with others.

[II, 3723-5]

We're quite addicted to subtle discussions;
we're very fond of solving problems.
So that we may tie knots and then undo them,
we constantly make rules for posing the difficulty
and for answering the questions it raises.
We're like a bird which loosens a snare
and then ties it tighter again
in order to perfect its skill.
It deprives itself of open country;
it leaves behind the meadowland,
while its life is spent dealing with knots.
Even then the snare is not mastered,
but its wings are broken again and again.
Don't struggle with knots,
so your wings won't be broken.
Don't risk ruining your feathers
to display your proud efforts.

[II, 3733-8]

You are a bird of the sea,
even though a chicken has sheltered you beneath her wing.
The desire in your heart is for the sea;
your soul has that nature from your mother.
Leave your land-bound nursemaid and move on.
Come into the sea of reality.
You are a waterfowl:
you can live on land and sea.
You are of royal birth, for . . .
We have ennobled the children of Adam:
you walk on both dry land and sea.

[II, 3771-2]

Index

Poverty: I, 985; I 2373; I, 2834; II, 2963; II, 3472
Prayer: I, 381; I, 2625; II, 140; II, 339; II, 2769; II, 3537
Pride: I, 3240; I, 3245; I, 3347; II, 339; II, 3466; II, 3733
Prophet: I, 175; I, 381; I, 1141; I, 1319; I, 2521; I, 2653; I, 3086; I, 3460; I, 3555; II, 573; II, 600; II, 1876; II, 2732; II, 3013; II, 3036; II, 3242; II, 3411; II, 3500; II, 3549; II, 3598

Q
Qur'an: I, 1311

R
Righteousness: I, 2580
Rose: I, 2021; II, 153; II, 278; II, 1244; II, 1379; II, 2443; II, 3242

S
Saint: I, 714; I, 1947; I, 2521; I, 2602; I, 2873; I, 3086; I, 3255; II, 1938; II, 2153; II, 2163; II, 2346; II, 3108
Sea: I, 1647; I, 1743; II, 566; II, 939; II, 1028; II, 2811; II, 3140 II, 3278; II, 3371
Self: I, 772; I, 2195; I, 3004; I, 3460; II, 1175; II, 2325
Senses: I, 1126; I, 3099; I, 3180; I, 3562; I, 3775; II, 710; II, 1286; II, 3236; II, 3240; II, 3242; II, 3326; II, 3500; II, 3549
Separation: I, 3240; II, 186; II, 339; II, 1752; II, 2180; II, 3514
Shaikh: II, 1323; II, 1587; II, 3343
Sincerity: I, 866; II, 573; II, 2900; II, 3709
Soul: I, 149; I, 180; I, 760; I, 821; I, 1783; I, 1824; I, 2235; I, 2302; I, 2829; I, 3692; I, 3213; I, 3347; II, 729; II, 739; II, 746; II, 846; II, 1023; II, 1183; II, 1286; II, 1303; II, 1376; II, 1948; II, 2840; II, 2935; II, 2963; II, 3022; II, 3034; II, 3146; II, 3169; II, 3232; II, 3524; II, 3573; II, 3598; II, 3709; II, 3771
Spirit: I, 333; I, 409; I, 678; I, 723; I, 1743; I, 1976; I, 2006; I, 2521; I, 2911; I, 3562; I, 3775; II, 12; II, 186; II, 263; II, 450; II, 455; II, 714; II, 1253; II, 2951; II, 3140 II, 3251; II, 3261; II, 3292; II, 3311; II, 3326; II, 3709
Sufi: I, 134; I, 3495; II, 159
Sun: I, 542; I, 723; I, 1941; I, 3555; I, 3775; II, 186; II, 3031; II, 3132

T
Thorns: I, 152; II, 278; II, 1240; II, 1244
Thought: I, 1141; I, 2909; I, 3144; I, 3221; I, 3492; II, 450; II, 971; II, 1029; II, 1587; II, 1652; II, 3107; II, 3205; II, 3296; II, 3559
Truth: II, 1983; II, 2061; II, 2067; II, 2462; II, 2732; II, 2928; II, 2935

U
Unity: I, 3009; I, 3099; II, 2811
Universe: I, 2101; I, 2860

V
Vision: I, 921; I, 2133, I, 3756; II, 1975

W
Water: I, 817; I, 836; I, 866; I, 985; I, 1336; I, 3221; I, 3684; I, 3703; II, prologue; II, 418; II, 716; II, 1020; II, 1213; II, 1253; II, 1366; II, 1652; II, 1767; II, 1938; II, 2327; II, 2735; II, 2811; II, 2963; II, 3292; II, 3296; II, 3343; II, 3531
Wealth: II, 134; II, 371
Wings: I, 34; I, 866; II, 1042; II, 1264; II, 1552; II, 3733; II, 3771
Wisdom: I, 3255; II, 318; II, 1876; II, 3200; II, 3531
Women: I, 1494; I, 1783; I, 1824; I, 2425; I, 2437; I, 3448; II, 80
The Word: I, 34; II, 862; II, 971; II, 1323; II, 3292; II, 3542, II, 3573; II, 3598
Work: II, 734; II, 759; II, 971; II, 2429; II, 2443; II, 3022
the World: I, 79; I, 180; I, 215; I, 409; I, 523; I, 542; I, 982; I, 985; I, 1141; I, 1855; I, 2066; I, 2362; I, 2580; I, 2845; I, 3099; I, 3684; I, 3756; II, 11; II, 72; II, 153; II, 159; II, 466; II, 682; II, 703; II, 880; II, 1000; II, 1020; II, 1023; II, 1029; II, 1034; II, 2153; II, 2429; II, 2593; II, 2939; II, 3022; II, 3108; II, 3140; II, 3200; II, 3240; II, 3315; II, 3475; II, 3497; II, 3549; II, 3612